Dear Parent:

Congratulations! Your child is taking the first steps on an exciting journey. The destination? Independent reading!

STEP INTO READING® will help your child get there. The program offers five steps to reading success. Each step includes fun stories and colorful art. There are also Step into Reading Sticker Books, Step into Reading Math Readers, Step into Reading Phonics Readers, Step into Reading Write-In Readers, and Step into Reading Phonics Boxed Sets—a complete literacy program with something to interest every child.

Learning to Read, Step by Step!

Ready to Read   Preschool–Kindergarten
• big type and easy words • rhyme and rhythm • picture clues
For children who know the alphabet and are eager to begin reading.

Reading with Help   Preschool–Grade 1
• basic vocabulary • short sentences • simple stories
For children who recognize familiar words and sound out new words with help.

Reading on Your Own   Grades 1–3
• engaging characters • easy-to-follow plots • popular topics
For children who are ready to read on their own.

Reading Paragraphs   Grades 2–3
• challenging vocabulary • short paragraphs • exciting stories
For newly independent readers who read simple sentences with confidence.

Ready for Chapters   Grades 2–4
• chapters • longer paragraphs • full-color art
For children who want to take the plunge into chapter books but still like colorful pictures.

STEP INTO READING® is designed to give every child a successful reading experience. The grade levels are only guides. Children can progress through the steps at their own speed, developing confidence in their reading, no matter what their grade.

Remember, a lifetime love of reading starts with a single step!

To Heidi Kilgras—so smart, so fun,
so enthusiastic, and always a pleasure
—S.E.G. and M.J.D.

Acknowledgments: Our thanks to all the wonderful owners and drivers who helped us win our own monster truck race—the people at Bigfoot 4x4, Inc., especially Bob Chandler, Sr., Bob Chandler, Jr., Dale Runte, and Larry Swim; Mark and Tim Hall of Hall Brothers Racing; Doug and Brenda Noelke and Dale Gerding of Big Dawg 4x4; Jim Koehler, Chris Bergeron, and Stephanie Cotnoir of Avenger Racing; Pat Summa of Thrasher Motorsports; and Michael and Denise Vaters of Black Stallion 4x4. We also appreciate Russ Richey and the team at Family Events for their help in Lima, and Ross Bonar of TheMonsterBlog.com for his support.

Finally, thanks to Heidi Kilgras, Chelsea Eberly, and Marianna Smirnova of Random House, who brought us over the finish line.

Photo credits: pp. 4–6, 25, 29: © BIGFOOT 4x4, Inc.; pp. 7, 47: © Kenneth Sundström; pp. 9, 11 (bottom): © Stephanie Cotnoir; pp. 12–13: © Russ Richey, Family Events; p. 27: © John Keller of 3778 photography, courtesy of Quick Motorsports; p. 28: © Denise Vaters.

Visit us on the Web!
www.stepintoreading.com
www.randomhouse.com/kids

Educators and librarians, for a variety of teaching tools, visit us at
www.randomhouse.com/teachers

Library of Congress Cataloging-in-Publication Data
Goodman, Susan E.
Monster trucks! / by Susan E. Goodman; photographs taken and selected by Michael J. Doolittle.
  p. cm.
ISBN 978-0-375-86208-3 (trade) — ISBN 978-0-375-96208-0 (lib. bdg.)
1. Monster trucks—Juvenile literature. I. Doolittle, Michael J. II. Title.
TL230.5.M58 G66 2010   796.7—dc22   2009031852

Printed in the United States of America   20 19 18 17 16 15 14 13

Monster Trucks!

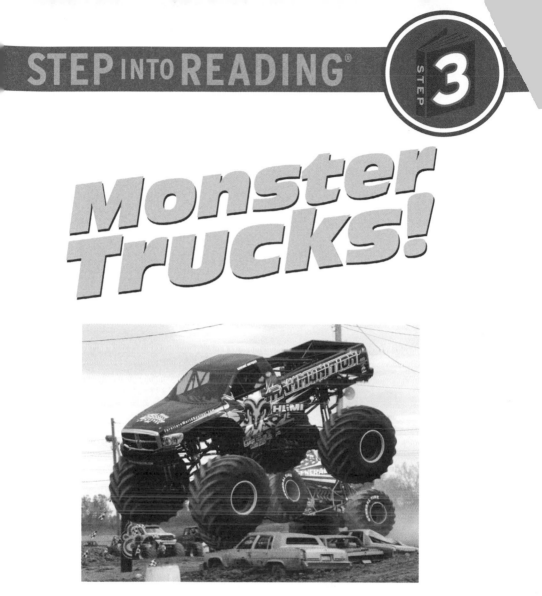

By Susan E. Goodman
Photographs taken and selected
by Michael J. Doolittle

Random House 🏠 New York

A Monster Truck Is Born

Bob Chandler loved his

pickup truck.

He liked driving it

over rocks and mud.

Bob got bigger tires

so he could do that.

Then Bob thought the truck

needed more power.

He added a bigger engine.

Bob kept making
his truck bigger and stronger.
That's how the first
monster truck was born!
Bob named it Bigfoot.
He took Bigfoot to car shows.
Fans loved this
super-sized machine.
Soon other people began building
monster trucks of their own.

Then Bob had a new idea.

He drove his truck

over some old cars.

Bigfoot flattened them

into a car pancake!

The crowds loved it!

Monster trucks had a new trick.

Before long,

people started to race

monster trucks.

The trucks were already strong.

Now they had to be fast, too.

Some trucks have crazy names,
like Nitemare, The Crash Master,
and Towasaurus Wrex.
Some are painted to look like
wild creatures.
But they all roar like monsters!

Look What These Monsters Can Do!

Monster trucks are amazing.

They are very heavy.

Yet they can jump more than

twenty feet in the air.

Huge motors help them fly.

These motors can be

six times more powerful

than a car engine.

They make a lot of noise, too.

Monster trucks can go fast.

They use a lot of fuel

when they race.

They burn almost

one gallon of fuel each second!

Monster trucks spin.

They plow through mud.

They roll over cars

and crush them like bugs.

They usually ride on

four wheels.

At times they use just two.

Sometimes a truck comes down
from a jump too hard.
This one lost a wheel!

Don't worry!

The crew can fix

almost anything.

What Makes It
a Monster?

A monster truck IS a monster.

It is huge.

It weighs about 10,000 pounds.

That is as heavy as

an elephant.

Its tires are huge, too. They are at least sixty-six inches high. Each one can weigh 900 pounds.

Here are the parts of a monster truck:

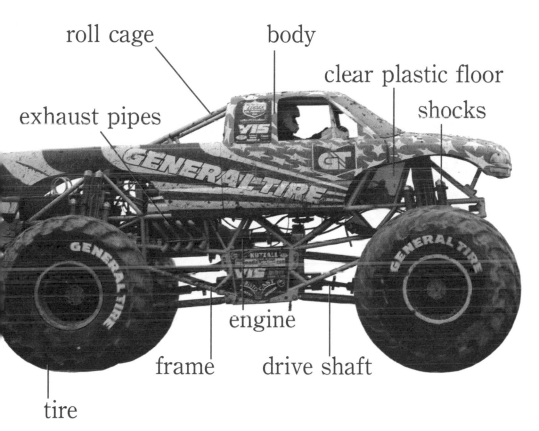

roll cage   body

clear plastic floor

shocks

exhaust pipes

engine

frame   drive shaft

tire

Here is a monster truck
frame without the body:

Monster trucks make many jumps.

They go over lots of bumps.

Cars and trucks have

parts called shocks.

The shocks soften the ride.

Monster trucks need

super shocks!

A special gas pedal keeps

the driver's foot in place

during bumpy rides.

Look closely at a
monster truck.

The body is all one piece.

Its doors and headlights

are not real.

They are just painted on.

The steering wheel
turns the front tires.
Drivers have a special lever
to steer the back ones.

lever

This helps the truck
make tighter turns.

Racing can be dangerous.

So monster trucks have

extra safety features.

A metal roll cage

protects the driver

if the truck tips over.

Drivers wear

five-point safety belts.

A fire extinguisher

is kept close by

in case there is a problem.

Clear plastic floors
also help drivers stay safe.
Monster trucks are so tall
that drivers cannot see the track
right in front of them.
They need to know
if it is clear
to come down from a wheelie.
So they look through
their floors to find out!

The Biggest and the Best

Monster truck drivers

like to set records.

So they try new tricks.

In 1999 Bigfoot tried a stunt

never done before.

Monsters had jumped over cars.

They had sailed over trucks.

This time Bigfoot would

fly over a plane!

Bigfoot's engine roared.

Driver Dan Runte had to go
at least sixty miles an hour
to make it over the jet.
He raced up the ramp
faster than that.
Bigfoot soared into the air
and over the jet!

Bigfoot set two records that day.
Dan set a new monster truck
speed record by going
almost seventy miles an hour.
And Bigfoot jumped 202 feet!

Dan Runte—record-breaking driver

Another time,
Ghost Ryder did
the first backflip
ever completed at a show.

Black Stallion was the first
to fly over a moving target.
Monster trucks often jump cars
that are standing still.
This red monster was driving
right at Black Stallion!

Bigfoot 5 is the world's tallest
monster truck.
Its tires are ten feet tall!

Stunts and records are great.
But many people
love races the best.

Getting Ready
for a Show

The show starts tomorrow.

Thrasher's crew gets ready to go.

Crews sometimes travel

hundreds of miles to compete.

That is a lot of driving

to race for just a few minutes!

Monster trucks are not allowed
to drive on public roads.
They must ride in trailers.
But they are too big to fit in.
So drivers replace
the giant tires
with smaller ones.

Then they drive the truck in.
They also pack spare parts.
Racing causes a lot of
breakdowns!

At the track, workers are busy.

They are preparing the course.

Forklifts stack cars in a pile.

Bulldozers push dirt into

mounds.

Trucks pack the dirt down.

They are making strong ramps

so the monsters can fly!

The drivers arrive and
unload their trucks.
They put the big tires back on.
They make sure everything
is working right.

Then they wash their trucks down.

The monsters
and their drivers
are ready to star
in their show.

It's Showtime!

The monster trucks rumble
onto the track.
The crowd cheers.
It is time to race.

Monster trucks race

two at a time.

Each pair lines up side by side.

The drivers rev their engines.

The crowd begins

the countdown.

". . . three, two, one, GO!"

The trucks soar over
the first ramp.

They fly over the second one.

They hit the third at full speed.

These trucks get a lot
of air time!

Freestyle time is another part
of the show.
The drivers do whatever stunts
they want.
Big Dawg crushes the vans.

Avenger is going to jump high.

The driver straightens the tires.

When the wheels hit the cars,

the driver guns the motor.

Up it goes!

General Tire does a "donut."
This means that the truck
drives in small circles.
The driver steers
the front tires
to the left.

He uses his lever to turn

the rear tires

to the right.

The monster truck goes

round and round.

Look at that mud fly!

The monster trucks are done.

But the next event is fun, too.

The drivers come out

to be with their fans.

This show is over.

There will be another soon.

Over 12 million people

go to monster truck shows

each year.

Monster trucks race

all over the world!

That's because they are
monstrously fun!